Forgotten Steam
Photographed by Nick Nicolson
Compiled by Ron White

© Images and Design: The Transport Treasury 2021. Text: Ron White

ISBN 978-1-913893-11-8

First published in 2021 by Transport Treasury Publishing Ltd. 16 Highworth Close, High Wycombe, HP13 7PJ
Totem Publishing, an imprint of Transport Treasury Publishing.

www.ttpublishing.co.uk

Printed in Malta By Gutenberg Press

'Forgotten Steam' is one of a series of books on specialist transport subjects published in strictly limited numbers and produced under the Totem Publishing imprint using material only available at The Transport Treasury.

Front Cover: It just had to be something Great Western; something successful in it's day (even if not quite as quick as Rous-Marten would have us believe). Swindon really made a job of her, she looked well, went well on her daily trips to Southampton via Newbury and shared the work with an LSWR Greyhound from Eastleigh, sizzling gently in the background. The third loco is No. 6304, one of several hundred Moguls which were to be found anywhere on the Western on freight or passenger; suitable for cannibalisation when funds were tight in the 30s!
3 April 1957

Rear Cover: The massive bridge at Connel Ferry, one of two on the Ballachulish branch - the Victorians were convinced that remote communities should be connected to the main system and that they might make money from so doing.
September 1958

Frontispiece: The very first picture Nick took on his lovely new Retina 1a (and what a leap from an Ensign Selfix!) - the exposure wasn't perfect but it is sharp which is more than I could say of my first shot! 5026 CRICCIETH CASTLE has an up slow waiting in Reading station.
3 April 1957

Opposite: 2. Then he went next door to the Southern (on whom the Western, up above, looked down upon in every way) The shed there became with Guildford, a safe refuge for the elderly; last survivors and the sick and lame, I loved it as you might imagine. G6 No. 30277 must be shed pilot, what line duty could they find for her? 3 April 1957

Foreword

I little thought when I first offered my geriatric services to the publisher that he would listen to such a wild flight of fancy, but he did and "Steam in South Africa" has appeared (to my delight, and, I hope, his). Moreover, he has produced further collections of slides lying fallow and wonders if I could again make straw without bricks from a collection having no central theme, the work of a professional railway employee who took what he could when he could, plus railway holidays with companions (including Roy Vincent on a Scottish bash).

Nick Nicolson's output was richly varied, as were his cameras, starting with a Kodak Bantam, then an Ensign Selfix using 828 roll film (I've seen none of these!) to Kodachrome 1 35mm through a Retina1a in 1957/58. Sadly he went on to other cheap, but not cheerful films up to 1962, thereafter back to large format.

What you will see is most of what he took in 1957/58, apart from a trip to Ireland in June, and various industrial sites, both standard and narrow gauge, deliberately omitted. This is a walk down memory lane (if you're prepared to push my wheelchair); every jolt will dislodge something from the dark recesses of my mind until we reach that comforting conclusion of nearly every entry in the wonderful Shed Directory - "where a cinder path leads to the shed".

Ron White, Chesham
January 2021

3. (Left) Swiftly to Didcot for another shot of No. 3440 but consider instead her companion, surely the only loco designed verbally - Holcroft was told to "get me out a 2-6-0 with 5' 8" wheels, outside cylinders, the No. 4 boiler and bring in all the standard details you can". This didn't produce a Cruft's champion, more a touch of what you might expect from spontaneous combustion in a public park, a locomotive but not necessarily what had been expected, reliable plodders but iffy steamers when pushed as the No. 4 was on the small size.
3 April 1957

4. (Above) Westbury's 6955 *Lydcott Hall* finds herself on an Oxford - Paddington slow and looks well. When No. 2925 *Saint Martin* was rebuilt into No. 4900 and given 6' 0" drivers it also got "a luxury cab" - a statement given with a perfectly straight face. Never before or since could a side window and tip-up wood seats mounted so high that hardly anyone's boots touched the floor be so described: all Swindon's geese are swans as someone (not me) once said.
3 April 1957

5. A visit to Swindon Works soon followed, no actual date given. 3MT No. 82030 appears to be a brand new alien landed.

6. No. 1020 *County of Monmouth* in original single chimney form looks superb and will sound even better when put to a bit of hill climbing the short double chimney wrecked their looks whatever it did for steaming.

7. For most visitors what was waiting for attention or scrapping was of greater interest. TaffVale No. 397 looks well and might have found a niche as works shunter.

8. No. 3100 looks doomed; one of five No. 3150 class tanks rebuilt in 1938 with 3" smaller diameter drivers, a moderately futile exercise as tyre wear over the years would give much the same result.

9. Storm clouds gather behind *Dukedog* No. 9025, one of those with a tapered chimney and top-feed boiler - the least standard class over to emerge from that home of orthodoxy - but where else could you put together 29 locos from bits lying around the place?

10. Nick was certainly anxious to keep the Retina warm and almost immediately set sail for Scotland - how he got there I don't know but it was almost certainly by rail. His first shot was at Ayr shed and was unexpectedly an NBR Y9 pug No. 68118.
18 April 1957

11. (Left) On the following day Yoker offered the Caley equivalent with No. 56039 - handy little devices for getting into odd corners.
19 April 1957

12. (Above) Off to the far north and the delightful works at Inverurie where NBR J37 No. 64572 gleams and a full tender is a good sign.
20 April 1957

13. At Ferryhill it had to be A2 No. 60532 *Blue Peter* - the days of the A4s were but a dream and it was then, a bit mundane.
20 April 1957

14. Kittybrewster however was always worth a call, a friendly place where locos might be moved on request as was Z5 No. 68192; woken from sleep in the roundhouse. 20 April 1957

15. (Left) Another look at the charming little Manning Wardle tank and the kindly crew who did the necessary with their Jumbo.
20 April 1957

16. While you're about it, how about shifting GNSR D41 No. 62264? This elegant old soul was approaching her 60th birthday but hadn't long to live.
20 April 1957

17. Roy Vincent was certainly with Nick at Keith shed where they both took K2 No. 61783 *Loch Sheil* (which should have been *Loch Shiel*) - you don't get many wrongly spelt plates, I can only think of two others, a *Hall* and a *King Arthur*; plus a *Star* and a *K4* which were altered and recast after complaints!
20 April 1957

18. A strenuous day took them to Forres where the pilot was *Caley* 0-4-4T No. 55178 in fine nick. I'm not sure about her chimney (or lum in the vernacular) - her stovepipe has been capped by what might be an NBR device, it looks a bit lopsided.
20 April 1957

19. Eventually they got to Inverness where they found strength to climb the hill behind the shed and get this steamy panorama looking north as two Black 5s pass the coaling plant as they take off for Perth and, maybe, England.
20 April 1957

20. Turning west we see the splendid roundhouse and arched entrance which incorporated the water tank; the later brutal concrete of the coaling plant loses Brownie points.
20 April 1957

21. A closer look at the arch with No. 44925 brewing up - it must have been a long day for them and their cameras.
20 April 1957

22. The following day offered them a nice clean Caley Jumbo, No. 57607, said to be at Hamilton, a shed I never got to for unknown reasons.
21 April 1957

23. Eastfield shed served Queen Street station and provided power for the West Highland line, suburban services to Helensburgh/Craigendoran and a welter of lines north and east. D11/2 62682 HAYSTOUN OF BUCKLAW simmers, not initially welcomed for too many GCR foreign features but they ran like deer once their little ways were discovered; the GNR J50/2 No. 68957 alongside would have been equally cursed for HER sins.
22 April 1957

24. Has Caley No. 56321 been through Cowlairs works rather than St. Rollox to appear at NBR Eastfield? 60 years on, we'll never know.
22 April 1957

25. Nick's notes say that NBR J35 No. 64531 is passing an unknown shed but I seem to recollect seeing this in print somewhere and it said Motherwell - the industrial grot in the far distance is another clue.
23 April 1957

26. Ploughing homewards they took the air at Beattock where the pilot, 0-4-4T No. 55232 is propelling a small freight, brake van leading; could be the Moffat branch job as the far right arm of the bracket signal is off? Sheer guesswork on my part, I was last there in 1964 concentrating on tape recording!
23 April 1957

27. A dart out to Kingmoor found 46227 *Duchess of Devonshire* coaled high and readied for the up Royal Scot, not due for a while as she is boxed in by Britannia No. 70028 ROYAL STAR.
23 April 1957

28. Back to Citadel where a shiny new DMU would take them on via detour round the coast to Wukkinton (Workington) via Spaatry (Aspatria) - Cumbrian could be an impenetrable dialect!
24 April 1957

29. Although the DMU went on to Whitehaven. Ken (who may by now have been on his own) stepped off at Workington to do the shed, only No. 46457/89 outside.
24 April 1957

30. Thence to Manchester on a wearisome stopper headed by No. 44904 on a motley collection of stock.
24 April 1957

31. On arrival at Manchester he managed to get into Patricroft shed, where Jubilee No. 45558 *Manitoba* looks bright and cheerful; like the Castles, they varied immensely in virility.
24 April 1957

32. Also at Patricroft was LNWR G1 No. 49209 whose splendid ONE/TWO/three/fo.. beat was known and loved; never insulted with a smokebox numberplate; characterful.
24 April 1957

33. Rowsley offered a clean 8F No. 48176 - the shed was demolished, consumed by the jungle and is now being exhumed by the locals for future bright ideas.
24 April 1957

34. A view of Colnbrook station with an AEC railcar in blood and custard livery waiting to leave for West Drayton. The post and net to catch the tablet is conspicuous by the signal box which guards the level crossing.
May 1957

35. Pannier No. 9781 has a work train between Colnbrook and Staines West.
May 1957

36. Another shot of the work train approaching Staines West; the gang have spotted Nick and want to be in the shot.
May 1957

37. Staines West station, once a private house with T 572 waiting but sadly not providing a connecting service to anywhere. We had much to learn on the subjects of integrated transport and/or duplication of services by road and rail.
May 1957

38. N15X No. 32331 BEATTIE has arrived at Windsor & Eton Riverside with a special from London via a most devious route. Rebuilds of LBSCR 4-6-4 tank engines they were intended to work on the same rosters as the King Arthurs but they preferred the quieter life that Basingstoke shed could provide.
23 June 1957

39. Black Motor No. 30692 had been sent to Windsor to help shuffle the stock - the stark LSWR outline shrieks against the N15X elegance.
23 June 1957

40. Up the hill, outside the castle was, of course, the Great Western with No. 6122 ready to go to Paddington, the station remains but much reduced in size and commercialised. All 70 of the 61xxs were once allocated to PDN, SHL,SLO & RDG (81A/B/C?D in metric) to cover the whole suburban service which they did, admirably.
23 June 1957

41. 'Get orf my land" was the cry in 1872 when the Watlington & Princes Risborough Railway appeared outside the gates of Shirburn Castle and the station had to be built a long way from the town; 60 odd years after closure the remains still survive, just.
29 June 1957

42. No. 4650 has arrived quietly with a morning train, the frantic and false jollity of the afternoon and evening is to come The stark carriage shed is behind the loco.
29 June 1957

43. A better view of the station and the first family has the bench to themselves.
29 June 1957

44. No. 4650 has unhooked and run round the coach to the parachute tank for some chalky water; there had been a loco shed at the Chinnor end of the station but it burned down in 1905 and the lonely passed cleaner/fireman on the night shift was condemned to spend the night in a converted horsebox after he had blacked in the fire and filled the boiler. Once the horsebox had been condemned; the loco and crew left Slough shed at 05.56 to get to Watlington by 07.00.

45. (Left) The crowds (and clouds) gather in the afternoon; I had intended to be there but had to attend a wedding instead, a poor substitute. Peter Handford of Transacord Records was there and I still have his 10" LP which has caught not only the uproar but also the gentleness of the line as it normally was.
29 June 1957

46. (Right) Lewknor Bridge Halt; the first stop out of Watlington was not opened until 1906 and, although close to the village, the locals preferred the buses, such as there were. One or two bodies have appeared.
29 June 1957

47. Aston Rowant station was identical to Watlington and Chinnor and was close to the main A40 to Oxford; No. 4650 calls on the last morning.; who will tend the rambling roses and raise water by the hand pump on the end wall?
29 June 1957

48. No. 4650 has had a busy day and has the very last scheduled service, a second coach had to be added to carry all the people who never dreamt of using the line in real time. It was a pity Nick never got any pictures at Chinnor which was the hub of the line then, as it is again now, in preservation, with the perfect replica station but not the cement works which appeared in 1921 and closed in 1989.
29 June 1957

49. Had I been there, I would have caught this Marylebone train to get to High Wycombe where I would have caught a 362 bus to Chesham (it went on to Ley Hill in those days). Subsequently I cycled to Risborough to see Peter Handford and buy his latest record, I started with his 78 rpm shellac disc of steam on the GC (7/6d = 37 1/2p) - he only made 99 copies to avoid paying tax!) - wrapped it in whatever, put it in my saddlebag (remember them?) and hoped it would survive. It did, I've stlll got it AND the one with the Lickey Banker at work (I contrived to footplate 58100 when I was doing my square-bashing at Bridgnorth in 1950 so I had to get that one as well). The L1s were going to revolutionise the GC and replace my beloved A5s - instead they knocked themselves to pieces in no time flat, caused men to lose their jobs or resign, and shook dentures out of driver's mouths, they were known as "concrete mixers" and not affectionately either. 29 June 1957

50. I 'm going to have to cheat and use a couple of mine, but Marylebone was mentioned and much has been said of her - Betjeman, in his early days described it "like a branch library in a superior Manchester suburb" but A G Macdonell in 1933 went overboard - "……quietest and most dignified of stations, where the porters go on tiptoe, where the barrows are rubber-tyred and the trains sidle mysteriously in and out with only the faintest of toots upon their whistles so as not to disturb the signalmen…………" That might have been true in 1933 when the A5s monopolised things and the GCR low pitched whistle was easy on the ear; and easy on the eye as well, for Robinson, the CME of the Great Central only produced one ugly locomotive, his 2-6-4 tanks which became class L3.

51. By 1957 the L1s were falling to bits, clanging and screeching their way to an early grave; but one could still keep dry under the porte-cochere should one be brave enough to enter what had been the hotel, but which had become "the Kremlin" home to the top BR brass hats. Now, once again it is a luxury pad, 5 stars, top whack and Marylebone still is a railway, not a coach station.

52. Out into the wilds of Kent, where the East Kent Railway went from Shepherdswell to nowhere in search of coal and passengers, they found the former, but not the latter and not enough of either. With immense optimism they carved the Golgotha Tunnel for double track, but never need more than one: O1 No. 31065 emerges with a special near closing time, Nick didn't record the date and I can't remember.

53. A call at Folkestone Harbour produced what is described as a Boat Express; the third vehicle is a Cafeteria Car, was this normal on the regular services? An R1 tank sets off up the 1 in 30 gradient off the end of the swing bridge for a steady plonk up the hill.
July 1957

54. This must have been something odd since only two locos can manage the train, three or four were generally needed and the little shed behind the down platform at the Junction station was always busy.
July 1957

55. Nick started his BR employment on the Southern in Orpington Control and so we can enjoy a trip around Hampshire and the Isle of Wight starting at Basingstoke where Urie N15 No. 30748 *Vivien* was receiving attention - just look at the length of that clinker shovel (or paddle) leaning against the cab; it wasn't all glamour at the front end.

56. On to Fratton, one of the less photographed sheds as the Portsmouth line was electrified pre-war. The place was busy enough when he called and T9 No. 30288 looks as fit as a flea.
18 August 1957

57. No. 76067 is nearly new, and looks very well with the larger tender, alongside Urie H15 No. 30487 carries a SPL 8 disc and the head code lamps for Waterloo - Portsmouth Harbour via Eastleigh.
18 August 1957

58. *LBSCR* E4 No. 32479 is clean and comely but what did she do?
18 April 1957

59. U class No. 31794 was one of the first batch rebuilt from the K class 2-6-4 tanks, one of which came off at speed near Orpington and caused a mighty flap at HQ. These were good solid lumps and were around to the end, but not looking like this; they, and the Ns were notorious for turning brown from thrown rust and track debris.
18 August 1957

60. I thought this was an N when I saw the tiny splasher, but no, another U from the second batch showing detail differences - this was the last in service, 31639. Both have their original front ends and chimneys and look all the better for them.
18 August 1957

61. Fratton's residents to the end of steam were the delicious little Brighton Terriers, the oldest, lightest and daintiest of machines to be found on BR and retained so that creaking Langstone Bridge might survive a while longer. No. 32661 is one of about a dozen spread between here and Newhaven plus the Brighton Works pet.
18 August 1957

62. BB Class No. 34051 *Winston Churchill* **looks a bit rugged on Fratton, note the red backed nameplate, all BBs subsequently went pale blue and only the WCs retained red.**
18 August 1957

63. BB Class No. 34051 almost immediately went off shed to go to Eastleigh and Nick went with her/him for the ride; on arrival he realised that all had not gone well, and the "air-smoothed" casing (to quote OVS) was cockled from an earlier lagging fire. Locos often ran like this, but 34051 was earmarked for the National Collection and had to be flattened.
18 August 1957

64. A closer look at the original tender showed a few faults as well as a good look at the first BR totem, received with a volley of abuse.
18 August 1957

65. The *Nelsons* were handsome beasts but needed understanding with their long grates and only when Stephen Townroe got his hands on them at Eastleigh for the boat trains did we see what they could do. No. 30863 *Lord Rodney* is coaled high and ready to go.
23 August 1957

66. No. 30855 *Robert Blake* looks even better, little did we imagine the state BR would be in ten years hence.
23 August 1957

67. The Isle of Wight railway was a time-warp, Victorian locos and rolling stock provided every service, trains connected with the paddle steamers and succeeding motor ships - as someone said "the hovercraft has developed by leaps and bounds which is what makes it horrible to travel in" O2 16 *Ventnor* at Ryde shed.
23 August 1957

68. Just across the tracks was the works where devoted craftsmen kept everything going - how could we dream they would keep the 1938 ex- Bakerloo electrics warm and mobile until 2020? They were much more at home with O2 31 *Chale* which still had another nine years in her.
23 August 1957

69. Amazing how such a tiny island should need two sheds to cover the work; but much had gone by 1957, and Newport was not what it was, and suffered the indignity of having all the O2s dumped there when steam finished. O2 28 *Ashey* (not an inappropriate name for a steam engine) rests on shed.
23 August 1957

70. Paddington station arches were still graced with the Great Western coat of arms - the railway had in theory gone in 1948 but not in Paddington where the managers stalked the powers of corridor (as Eric Morecambe once wonderfully said adding hastily "backwards") DOMINE DIRIGE NOS/VIRTUTE ET INDUSTRIA it said - Lord defend us/Honesty and hard work; noble sentiments irreverently translated as - God help us/hard work is killing us.

71. A C3 trolleybus No. 262 has arrived at Paddington from Uxbridge - what choice of routes there was - Metropolitan line/Piccadilly/Vine Street via West Drayton/High Street via Denham (although that one had gone many years ago leaving fragments of the station up in the air by a truncated viaduct where the intention had been to link High Street with Vine Street) Nick had by now rejoined the railways and was based at Paddington.
August 1957

72. A quick visit to Old Oak naturally found a King brooding between jobs; No. 6009 *King Charles II* had by then got his double chimney which spoiled his looks. August 1957

73. 6132 kept him company as Jeeves served Bertie Wooster, faithful, deferential, reliable, everything a good servant should be. Loved by their crews, when they were required to work from Marylebone to Risborough/Aylesbury with the L1s they screamed the place down and the acting shed master at Neasden borrowed 6129/6166 to comfort them. He even scraped the paint off the chimney cap and safety valve bonnet to make them sleep easily at night.
August 1957

74. 6963 *Throwley Hall* is a rum choice for the up Cathedrals Express flaunting the headboard as she passes Hayes, for so many years the home of HMV Records whose factory adjoined the line.

75. (Left Top) More jollifications as another branch - the Nickey Line (and how it got that name nobody can agree upon) - bites the dust. No. 43245, pride of St. Albans shed takes a breather in Redbourn station. The line took off at Harpenden Junction from the down fast line, so any train blocked all four tracks of the Midland main line as it went on or off the branch causing delays. Passenger traffic was never much but freight was, right to the end and the firm that used it regularly could not believe how anxious BR was to stop them from doing so. 13 October 1957

76. (Left Bottom) Arrival at Hemel Hempstead (Midland) caused a mighty throng of both passengers and residents to gather - the station was up above the main shopping area and about halfway between the old and new towns, but it was not the end of the line which dropped down the valley side and swung across it on a fine viaduct to Heath Park Halt, a timber shack close by the hotel of that name (now, also departed). I can only remember one other branch where the passenger service ended at a Halt and that was in Wales at Old Ynysybwl. But, behold, the half has not been revealed unto you - the track went on to Boxmoor Gas Works adjoining the WCML for coal traffic: now read on!!!!!! 13 October 1957

77. (Right) At Heath Park Halt we left our train perched up in the air, passengers came down wooden steps to road level. Single track, no loop, where to go? Incredibly one could reverse into Cottrell's Yard (where this picture was taken) and which lay at road level and was another source of coal traffic but NOT the major source of freight which came from Hemelite building blocks up near Godwin's on the outskirts of the town. They had extensive sidings and their own little diesel shunters - when BR took away the pick-up freight these staggered to and from the junction and the whole line became their private siding and they bought of all things, and it seems on sheer good looks, a Clayton Type 17 D8568 a right mechanical box of tricks which meant finding a fitter (ex Bedford) and driver (ex-St. Albans) to minister to it and BR would only allow access at the Junction between 01.00 and 04.30 - what a way to encourage traffic.
13 October 1957

78. The shape and sound of things to come - nearly - Gerry Fiennes would have loved a fleet of even bigger ones for the ECML. As it was, this prototype on display in darkest Battersea was immediately called the Ice-cream van - the go-faster whiskers were of the period but give the impression it is slowly being promoted from corporal to sergeant.
October 1958

79. Black 5 No. 44922 shuts off approaching Ach-na-Cloich station - the first shot I've ever seen there and there must be another from the other chap, whoever he was.
September 1958

80. Another shot of that magnificent road/rail bridge over Loch Etive built by optimists as well as fine engineers.
September 1958

81. Scenery, with train. No. 55208 approaches Ballachulish Ferry halt with the branch train - now swept away by progress, so-called. What would that running-in board fetch in auction? September 1958

82. A close-up of No. 55208 at Ballachulish, cleanish, reliable, unsung, the backbone of our railways. Flashy express locomotives we sought, but these outnumbered them and so many CMEs will be remembered not for their large but not necessarily good locomotives, but by such as this design, introduced in 1902. September 1958